Flirting with Owls

Flirting with Owls

Poems By

Kathleen Calby

*For Deidre,
All the best now
and in the future,
KCalby
2023*

© 2023 Kathleen Calby. All rights reserved.
This material may not be reproduced in any form, published,
reprinted, recorded, performed, broadcast,
rewritten, or redistributed without
the explicit permission of Kathleen Calby.
All such actions are strictly prohibited by law.

Cover design by Shay Culligan
Cover art *What Did Harry Eat?* by Jane Wilcoxson
jane@janewilcoxsonstudios.com

ISBN: 978-1-63980-336-1

Kelsay Books
502 South 1040 East, A-119
American Fork, Utah 84003
Kelsaybooks.com

For my family, by birth and chosen,
past and present, with abiding love.

Acknowledgments

A poet may work alone but also in community, if fortunate enough to find one. For that, I thank a number of people: Karen Luke Jackson, my always first reader, editor and finest promoter; Jessica Jacobs, my Gilbert-Chappell mentor, who set me on my path of deeper discovery; Eric Nelson, a terrific poet himself, teacher and editor, who molded this group of poems into a collection; Marion Starling Boyer, who has guided and encouraged my work and become a friend along the way; my Ohio writing group which has traveled with me since 2010; the 7 Poets Group, with a special shout out to Greg Lobas, who reviewed this collection in an early form; Aimee Nezhukumatathil, who suggested I publish a chapbook; Anne Kaylor, editor of *Kakalak,* who first believed in my work and published the poem "Flirting with Owls"; Jeff Alfier, editor of *San Pedro River Review,* who has generously suggested other publications for my work; and so many others who have encouraged me along the way. To Susan Hipp Lincoln Cordoba, wherever you are, for telling me I could write poetry at age 14. Finally, a big hug to my family who love me unequivocally.

Poems in this collection have appeared in the following journals:

Broad River Review: "Harvest of Ice" (Rash Awards Poetry Finalist 2022)
Great Smokies Review: "Navy Boys: Montrose, Pennsylvania, 1942"
Hermit Feathers: "Geisha in the Woods," "Like Midas," "Refuge in a Bamboo Grove"
Kakalak: "Flirting with Owls," "Breakneck Creek," "Pattern of Enchantment," "Cider Press" (Honorable Mention 2020)
New Millennium Writings: "Mercy and 98 Other Names"
New Plains Review: "Visible"
Pinesong Awards Anthology: "Garden Tender," originally titled "Whose Garden Is It?" (Honorable Mention 2021)

San Pedro River Review: "The Shape of Kindness," "Night Kitchen"
Slippery Elm Literary Journal: "Bitters"
Soundings East: "Once Upon Seeking Narcissus"
Suisun Valley Review: "Storkbite," "Thieving Blackberries"
Susurrus: "Waiting for Rain's Perish"
Willows Wept Review: "Committed to Memory," "Tonight we pause"
Witness: Appalachia to Hatteras: "Cider Press," "In the meadow of later years," "Consider the Mountains," "The Shape of Kindness"

Contents

Visible	11
Harvest of Ice	12
Once Upon Seeking Narcissus	14
Navy Boys: Montrose, Pennsylvania, 1942	16
Cider Press	18
Breakneck Creek	20
Crown of Evening	21
In the meadow of later years,	22
Refuge in a Bamboo Grove	23
A breeze down the mountains	25
Geisha Among the Woods	26
Like Midas	27
Bitters	28
Night Kitchen	29
Storkbite	30
Tonight we pause	31
Consider the Mountains	32
Once Near Crater Lake	33
Thieving Blackberries	34
Numbered Days	35
Garden Tender	36
Pattern of Enchantment	37
Waiting for Rain's Perish	38
Vigil	39
Mercy and 98 Other Names	40
Committed to Memory	41
The Shape of Kindness	43
A Surface Disturbed	44
Flirting with Owls	45

Visible

Last night's rain reveals what might be
        unseen. Airlike threads tethered only
                from roof to pink begonia—a high-wire act
        that drips crystals. Those gems, not the weaving,
                lead me to its center—a broad opening—
    where eight delicate legs did not pass,
did not pirouette nor stitch, but left
        a portal, through which to gaze or enter.
    I see into the future and back
                into memory. Both spacious. Both
        empty

        of regrets and promises. The view
            momentary, but enough.

        This space,
    this web, fragments by tomorrow or sooner,
torn, but not by my hand. The wind
                will catch it up in its palm, wave
        it into the world to which it opens,
    somewhere west where sky is as
            the space between this looming.

Harvest of Ice

The air sharp as ginger, breath
wisps like milkweed floss. Bundled in wool,
underwear to coats, men harness a horse
to a cutter—plow straight across the frozen lake.

Again and again,   till blocks move into a channel
where another with a gaff waits,   scuffs the snow
     with his boot: white flecks rise. Light barely
awake, yet teams   of men and horses begin
     to harvest ice.

As I scan the photographs now, I remember how
     I leaned on grandpa's chair for stories about ice
and Blackey the horse   that fell through and wasn't
     seen again. But the one he never told was how,
how in the world,   the ice houses burned one September.

In pictures, he and his brother Rohan   stand on Crystal Lake
     in winter. I knew the swing of skates on ponds, not the lug
and pull,   the gritted tooth of work in the cold.   Those barns
in the background, the ice houses,   stored blocks big as
     granite year round. Sepia   tones make ghosts of the men.

No empire, but grandpa and Rohan built
     a business with ice   as the 19th turned 20th century.
Demand grew, even in small towns and more in cities.
In Europe, World War One   gassed soldiers.   Electricity
     wired homes here   for new appliances.   Another war
simmered.   The ice houses burned   as 1939's fall began.

Tonight, I dream of the lake, the photo
     in my hand. I stand   where the men stood, pull
a matchbook   from my jeans, tear   one red fingernail
from the strip.   Strike it.   The edge of the picture curls
     with flame, blooms into smoke. Everything becomes
ash, everything   except the lake.
          The lake remains.

Once Upon Seeking Narcissus

—after "Personal Helicon" by Seamus Heaney

*As a child, they could not keep
me from wells.* Water called
like blood, summoned me from chair
or chore, and I would answer,
search for depths stone-laid.
As a child, I knew these
entrances of mirror.

Some places so familiar I walked
blind with my father's silk
tie around my eyes to find
earth's cavity that held sky
as a sliced shimmer.

Other openings I came upon by scent.
Algae emeralds that garnered
frogs would slow my steps,
to part the grass or scrub and plumb
a tunnel's dark fall with plucked stones,
and once I brought a rope
to take its measure dry to wet.

I did not lower myself, cautioned
as I'd been against such recklessness,
though I sought some image nonetheless.
With chest flat to the stone, my hands
against the lip, I leaned inward
to where my navel told me, no farther.

Below, a face I couldn't recognize
stared at me. What if I descended
for a closer look? But no.
I could hear my mother's cries, her keening
if they fished my body up. So, I stood,
lingered at the edge. In the distance, a dog
barked at someone in his field.

Navy Boys: Montrose, Pennsylvania, 1942

Uniforms in boxes land on her doorstep,
and she must have a photograph.

Upstairs, the radio blares a pitch,
a strike. She hears the stomp, the cheer.
She calls to them. The game snaps off.
Steps thunder stair treads. When they leave,
silence will drop its covers everywhere.

In homefront windows,
small white tasseled flags appear.
Every family's hearts revealed
as stars: one blue for each
who serves, one gold for each
dead. Three shine blue in her window.
The street hovers with stars.

Constellating her universe of war,
these boys, my father one of them,
stare into the cyclops' eye
of the future. But they don't know that
yet. It's just a camera, their father behind it.

She stands in the doorway, arms folded.
Her boys jockey for the sofa's seats. Nothing
can harm them, they believe. Her body shudders—
she has led them to that belief. She tries
a smile, but her lips are thin. She's seen
the newsreels, read the lists in print.

An image survives. She knows this,
but how to compare the weight of bones,
of flesh, to what does not age. No more
than paper developed in red light, silvered,
into black and white. Bodies that cannot
long be preserved, given another life—

as everything becomes paper—orders,
letters, reports. Her boys reduced flat
as an unimagined world.
Punches and play moments before
it was snapped—sailor collars not quite
straight, tie knots slack, lace curtains behind.
They want to go back to the radio's ball game
or ship out tonight. Three dark-haired Irish boys.

They have no pictures yet, but they will
as friends' torsos rip, arms detach, ships shroud
in smoke, lifeboats capsize, kamikazes dive,
shrieking as hornets, the smell as shells explode.
They will return, these oh-so-young men,
but not like this. Their eyes in the photo now
look as if silver dollars placed there, shine.

Cider Press

We would gather the overripe
Empires marooned in orchards,
hear their plop as we tossed
them in buckets that once
held five gallons of paint. Now,
we harvested the end of summer.

Yellow jackets buzzed about us,
sometimes swarming the apples
we wanted. We would kick
and scatter them, warning the kids
away as we picked our gelt.
But the small ones would
return, running in circles,
fly around us. Hum and buzz.

Shriek and squeal. Sun heating
our necks at the collar trace.
The honeyed smell of fruit rot
rising from the ground. Underfoot,
so slick, once, I slipped.
Someone grabbed my arm,
and we laughed as he pulled
me back from the mush.
This was the start of our fall.

For the day's sweat covered
us, and we could have drunk
that too. All in our twenties,
bandanas and cutoffs. Lugging
our pails back to the press, we could
smell the sweet juice running
as one man or another turned
the wheel a hard crank to the right
and again to the right and again.

Beers in the cooler nearby.
But we waited as our labor poured,
filling jugs and jars homeward bound.
The amber this day held.

Breakneck Creek

One can mourn what still runs—
my childhood and that creek,
its shallow murk and muck,
the stink of skunk
cabbage in spring, water lilies

that opened like moon faces,
dull brackish roots exposed
as heat dried the bed's width
by half. Plump bees piloting
to hives, a squirrel's rustle,
a fern as it began its arch

and scroll. All their industry
did not disturb me, content
under a beech to muse.
Elbow-propped on moss
littered in stray copper leaves.

Sometimes, I brought a pen
and a pocket notebook, but often
just my thoughts or a sandwich
on homemade bread and Mason jar
of milk. But somewhere, a catch.
I did not know it then.

Crown of Evening

This peach glory, light perfect
for the camera, not hot nor sharp
nor too diminished. Oblique,

it illuminates edges, the underside
of beech and maple foliage, ridges
in oak bark. I settle into the forest's

pews, as its congregation, too, waits
for this fold in the day, the curve
in the world's orbit

to bend light just so.
An intake of air, as branches
stir, and I breathe

coffee or myrrh. This light perhaps
a scent only to me, a hand's warm glide
on my arm. Sometimes, I rise

and leave when light wanes,
other times after full dark. Often, I do not
even enter, but turn,

knowing the border of awe
slices, rains, burns.

In the meadow of later years,

Hell bent its fire back. Before then, time branded
iron's taste on tongue. Heat too close for breath.
Hordes of bees blared about me. Twisted
roots knee-felled me. All the traps set, sprung.

Watched first my mother, then my father, die—I not
even forty when that six years began. Both deaths punctuated
and lengthened by surgeries, recoveries, diminishments. And
work, constantly work, calling me. Shouting to return
to the buzzing hive, but I could not always find
that path back. My brain froze, thawed, numb. I drove
in a smog of cracked clocks, cold coffee, sobbed breaths.

Then it was over. The graves covered. Stones set.

What happened next, I couldn't say. I worked, I droned,
never sipped the nectar I conveyed. Until the day I came
to a meadow. The grass long and bright
in its reaches. Sun soothing it like water. Breezes
lightly bowing it. My own buzzing stopped.

A fox stepped from the woods' edge, all sunhoney its fur,
small but teeth sharp. Neither of us to be misjudged in
a haloed field. The rings of hell dropped away. I forgot
the names for sin, which number as many as those
for god. I turned my head, blinked.

No pursuit or cover. The woods to our backs.
The infinitesimal rustle of field around our ears.
We let breeze take our flight and shadow, hint
at Queen Anne's lace, soft wood rot, fresh scat
nearby. Lifted our noses, our eyes,
to what rose beyond our reach.

Refuge in a Bamboo Grove

Canes clack and rattle
as I enter vertical lines
of light, then dark.
Cool here as leaves lace
a roof a story above me.

A cornfield when I was four
held stalks as tall as this.

Lost in a field, so green,
only slices of
sky showed through,
heat covered me, rose
from dirt mounded
in rows at my feet, and
where had my dad gone?

I didn't know to call, till
my voice hollered
"Dad! Dad! Dad!"

"Over here," came the reply,
though "here" a mystery
in this land of emerald poles,
shadowed leaves, golden tresses.

But his voice so easy,
I knew I would find him,
or he would catch me up
and lift me into the sky,
his hands rough, covered
with dirt, smell of tractor oil
on him, his shirt back damp.

Today, I seek relief
from a bleaching sun.
I want no one to find me.
My own hands rough now,
dirt seals the nails.

A breeze down the mountains

on a day that binds heat
to skin and holds tight
as arms locked around the chest
take all breath away,
someone offers a kind word,
thanks you for a small grace
you did not know you gave,
or opens a door.

A simple door. A real door.

A common gesture,
but more than enough
on a day when grief suffocates
and scalds the air
as it has for months,

and, just then, a breeze
moves down the mountains,
lets peace take its place.

Geisha Among the Woods

Certain as forsythia, shy
    as a doe, the dogwood,
        the understory,
takes the lead
            come April, when
she loosens blooms
before those higher branches
        block light
and offer her seclusion.

A geisha among the woods,
    too delicate for sun,
           her petals powdered pale.
    Dozens
of porcelain teacups
           balance on her arms.

A maiden's ghost
    skirting trunks,
        her white kimono
           netted in grapevine.

Like Midas

Sweet dust of day,
pollen goldens every
element in this atlas
of spring. Its fingers
touch and change even
those things I prefer
left undisturbed,
say, windshields
    or shoes forgotten
    outdoors.

Sweet dust covers
phlox in the beds.
Everywhere it lays
waiting to become
honey. Gilds lawn
chairs, yard toys, garden
hose: turns them
to bees' rapture and my
    unbecoming
    dismay.

Bitters

Smell of batwing hovers, a stew
bubbles on a hotplate in back. Shades
half-drawn, herbs dry from the rafters.

A haze rises from leftover cigarette
smoke, accumulated dust. Teas and spices
line the shelves. A bottle of vodka stands

off to the side, saved for tinctures, perhaps
the occasional drink. Hair cobwebbed
white, a woman tempts me to taste

a drop

she releases on my fingertip. I touch
to tongue. *Cardamom,* she whispers.
And alcohol fumes into my head

with the spice that triggers remembrance:
a bazaar in Luxor where saffron and silks
breezed my face, Abydos' gardens with pink

lotus bursting like pomegranates, the felucca's sail slap
and catch as boatmen call out, pull ropes that draw
the sky, always Egyptian blue, closer.

Bitters, she says. But I know
it all too sweet.

Night Kitchen

So late, the dark closes in on bedroom sheets slacked. The kitchen
becomes salvation: the dishes stacked,
     silverware placed
     just so, a fridge full of milk, fruit and eggs. New

worlds appear with chop, stir and knead. The rain nails
the roof in solid spikes. Perhaps that woke me,
     while all else slept,
     except the owls, raccoons and skunks who keep

these hours too. Or monks who chant and listen for response,
which may echo from Jupiter's moons. But who
     knows that except
     another mother in a kitchen with a hunger

to be satisfied by night's own invitation to this
white enameled stove that anchors the countertops
     and painted metal cabinets above
     that provide what's necessary,

as I prepare soups, pies and casseroles on the many nights
this place serves as the celestial body I turn to
     because no other now orbits these rooms
     or hallways. Because I need this sustenance of night.

Storkbite

for Christopher

Not a bruise, this red bloom around your eye
that opens bright blue in infant surprise.
I loved you more for that mark the stork left.

We all wanted you perfect, of course, counted
toes and fingers, heartbeat, your breath. Those
reassured us. The birthmark, a surprise, but
your jaundice tremored our blood. We clasped
hands beseeching your liver to be strong. Soon,
that saffron hue left but not the blushing petal.

It would likely disappear, doctors said. Likely,
but when? I knew a handsome man with such a mark
over half his face—a wine glass spill. Could never tell
if it made him more attractive or less.

Then, I wondered how he felt. Did he know
women wanted to blend their fingers with that Bordeaux
from temple to chin? Would others feel the same
for you? I couldn't be sure. I longed to show you
everywhere but knew I could not shoulder
glances cast aside, unasked advice.

You who emerged to rest in my arms, warmed
to show me the namelessness of stars,
the glow beneath an atom's skin. That passing
mark left when you were two, yet here I claim it
once again: I saw only you.

Tonight we pause

drunk, sordid   we do not stopper
    incandescence.   Instead, our draughts   ensure
blindness   to more celestial bodies.

We once knew   stars   constellations   ways
    that guided us   without compass.
Noted transits, disposition   right ascension
      consulted   the ephemeris for confirmation
which clarified   our own movements   our field of view.

What did Edison think   when he brought spark
    to filament   captured fire in a globe.   Had he never heard
 of Prometheus?   For a while   we called this   nightless day
     productive   safe.   We said it was good.

Glare   clutter   trespass: what light becomes
     as it bleaches   its absence. Our spurious   luster.
 We cannot net   this dark   again.

Consider the Mountains

Like the sparrow and the lilies,
they neither toil nor weep.
Although their stature and concerns
are larger, they do not carry heads that weigh
and weigh. They free themselves
of such mantles as leaky roofs,
mouths to feed, work to end. Trees grow
heavy with cones on their sides. Laurel
bloom and cause no sorrow
when they brown and drop. Ginger fox
and lumbering bear home in their dens.
The granite and greenness
do not hoard nor envy. They live
with the air being clean or not,
water as is, sides hewn or shaded.
They move slowly, rest a lot.

Once Near Crater Lake

The night abuzz with bats. No cave
in sight, the trees must house
their hangings. Drawn here

for postcard views, I stop at Becky's Diner,
no less famous—for pie. It's September,
thin poles fifteen feet high already line

the drive for the coming snowplows.
Everything starts to close next week,
the cashier says. *Snow can come*

early and heavy, but the lake never
freezes. My face begs the answer,
and she replies, *Too deep.* Like the night

sky here, and how dark has depth.
I take my plate, a slice of huckleberries,
outside to watch these aerialists,

try not to tempt them for a bite. None
come that close, although they swoop and
dive and nearly careen in the backdrop

of arc lights, then move into a depth
stars hardly pierce that would cover
me in pitch if I stepped anywhere

without a light beyond this range
of picnic tables and parking lot. Nearby,
Crater Lake, a blue eye, stares into space.

Thieving Blackberries

Everyone knows these small
questionable acts of conscience,
or its lack. The blackberries
are ripe now by the pond,
near houses but in no one's yard.

Accept my apology, false
as it is. I took one or two
handfuls and then another of these
bursting indigo beads that birds
were also scavenging as were bees.

I have braved the snares of thorn,
threat of hiss and sting for this prize.
Not for lack of want did I try
to withstand temptation, but
the taste so sweet, so warm.

Numbered Days

for Manu

When he is gone, the skateboard's click and whir
        will flee. Speed and spree dissolve.
                I do not want quiet
            to begin as shadow. It is already longing.

     Air will continue after this season, threshing its voice
  as wind. Fields will be gleaned. Frogs will dive
from the cold and vanish
      to reappear next spring.
          Screech and clack of board and wheels may not

       be heard again. Where will he go, this one, sleek
    as a hawk? Bolt from haven nest to thermals, preen
in oak heights, while I search for signs. I do not ride

      these currents as he does. Summer passes, his limbs
    lengthen and flap yet cannot gain the air
he wants. My bones know harvest as youth revel
in boundless, wanting only warmth enough to cast jackets
   off.

Garden Tender

Rusted rebar, a thread of sequins,
stray red bricks, broken necks
of beer bottles, a fluorescent
tennis ball chomped in halves.

Violets here grow beyond
their means; locust saplings shove
for sun, knock the leaves out
of others; wild strawberries scatter
their young and sprawl.

I crave order.
The young anarchist in me laughs.

I cannot do much for the world now
but rake, hoe, shovel
and plant. Cultivate and tend.

The rubber Godzilla stays.

Pattern of Enchantment

I rake leaves coiled
round an azalea pregnant
with bloom, bend to capture
those close to its roots. Twisted,
a piece of clothesline lies half
buried, gone brown then
black, then curls, slides
farther back, a tail slips
beneath   dark edges.

Back out it comes
to gauge my presence.
Diamonds
cross his back, his sides.
So small, so lithe,
he glides as a muscle
relaxed. Nothing
to shake, too young
for rattles' warning.
No tongue flicker or hiss.

Perhaps I misjudge
his species. I who
buckle with weight
from fear of snakes.
But   this   one
casts a spell, holds me
with his length and gaze.
No alarm takes

my breath nor brings my hand
for spade to strike. He
too young to do like.
We stare, take our measure,
untroubled.

Waiting for Rain's Perish

Torrent hushes hounds, children
curl and whimper. Sleep, we say,
though we lay wake side by side,

listen to rain's knife flicks
on roof, windows, house sides,
pray they not slice through.

For days, dawn sky bays low
to ground. Perpetual dusk.
Eggs, grits left untouched.

Walls damp, paper bubbles. Toilet
drips in answer. Cornmeal, sugar,
salt clump. Bread beards green.

All week rain stole land, spread into
yard. No boat, the car useless.
Water raised itself as it came down.

Carolina flood, it drowned
basement, skirted porch, took
branches, chickens, small rodents

surprised by its currents.
Moved on, they abandoned us.
No relief caught in sky's hand.

Only when night drums dark,
do we lose sight of damage, omens.
Pause, scared to be so blind.

In such poverty of light, we
pray for rain's perish,
silence with the ground again.

Vigil

        A candle will not make much

visible beyond a small circle—not
far larger than an arm's length.
It is light, but why place

our hopes on what we can see
when tragedy bashes
the door into splinters, knocking

    the frame apart, distorting
    what was closed to such reckless
    upheaval. What good
    a candle's flame then? No power

withstands
tragedy, not a man's hands,
well-built homes, border walls,
two towers, an earthen dam.

      Nothing is hard enough to brace

    against its barrage, so we must
        yield,
    soften the blow with what

    tenderness we possess. Women
      know this:
          muscles that cannot lift can hold

        another body
        in our arms.

Mercy and 98 Other Names

Carnations—given as apology, their petals
like scissored paper, their scent of clove—
placed in my hands from my lover who knows

how I will nestle my face in their cluster,
breathe in that request for forgiveness,
embrace kindness, knowing the need

for balance. How these thrived in what was
once Persia, and God's presence was fragrant,
before the wars bulleted and bombed such

beauty, before the women screamed
and men were hanged with their necks loose,
and all else dragged by gravity. What

has become of the faithful's gardens?
For those too were a prayer, and the Qur'an
praises them. Its verses of compassion

for widows and children, even non-believers.
Now, land mines bloom body parts. But
fountains still rise to mist the desert air

in home courtyards where carnations
and roses, fig trees and almonds, grow
in harmony and stature. A breeze drifts

some evenings, seduces the devout
to rise from their prayers and walk
into beauty and the non-believers

to pray. All fingering their beads for
God's names, which begin with mercy.
Even in rubble, the scent of clove endures.

Committed to Memory

You're in a garden. It's a cemetery. Flowers
bloom everywhere, even on bushes. But it is July,
not May when azaleas and rhododendrons would grace

the dead. You follow a name engraved in marble with
your index finger. It is not your name nor the name
of the man you're with, who turns you to kiss you.

"We can practice that," he says. "Of course," you laugh.
You know the dead are listening, perhaps watching, but,
most of all, remembering. You once thought the living

remembered the dead, but it's the other way around.
They commit every image, every word to memory,
so long you cannot imagine it. Nor can they. For they

no longer imagine anything. Yet they record,
like a camera without pause. You too are recording
this moment but do not have the memory of the dead.

You will have to ask them later. Much later, perhaps.
The light shimmers and glazes this man so he appears
more light, less body. The sun is so full, you can't

see him clearly, but you don't look away. What if,
when he turned you to kiss him, you had fallen? Here,
among so many buried. But he holds you. Then you recall

a young man who arrived here at eighteen. The silence
barely covers him. Now, beyond the garden's high bushes,
the cemetery's barrier, you hear the traffic. No accordion

of metal or glass occurs, just the hum of tires over blacktop.
You know where the young man lies. But you do not
want to remember that now. The dead will. You bow

your head into this man's shoulder. You want to be shrouded
in his warmth. That young man's body is closer to fields
of daffodils that bloom in spring. This man is nowhere

near those fields. Nor is it spring. It is no longer
summer either. Who remembers anything now?

The Shape of Kindness

Before I left, I took the snakeskin
from the desk to the woods. The one
found on our welcome mat, when
we had seen none live or coiled
in the yard. The one I kept, so I could
handle its skin.

I placed it near that bald
boulder, near the wild rose, near
the beech tree where robins
rest, down the slope from our once
bedroom window.

That day and next, I walked the land,
stroked the bark of trees, whispered
words to the creek, reluctant
to say goodbye to you and there.
Both good to me.

I couldn't confine that skin
to a shelf—have others regard it
as dead. It had breathed
life into me. Afraid as I was
of its brothers, it left only
what I could touch.

A Surface Disturbed

Water turns turns turns again. No eddy
on a lake does that. The surface
unsettled. A man with a camera calls me
over to talk about this spinning, how

*males, who've made their nests, now must lure
their mates to take a spin.* The water churns.
An emerald flash, then silver, a touch
of pink sapphire about the gills,

the largemouth bass leaps for an instant—
no more.
What a line this man casts. I could dive,
I can swim. What he does not capture

on film is the redbud behind us blooming,
the pears just past.

Flirting with Owls

No one would accuse the birds
with their raucous melodies,
rolling trills in upper scales
and sharp note reveilles
of being a public nuisance,
but, privately,
they are a bit early today.

For I have been flirting
with owls
deep in the muffled woods.
Air sharp as cinnamon,
my breath an apparition.
Hands warmed in gloves,
boots snug to socks.

Dusk feathered in,
and I, layered with down,
stayed watching
long after light left.
I could not tell you what
I stood to find
in such a cast of night.

But resting amid branches,
my eyes now useless, I turned
to listen,
present to octaves of silence,

which became wonder

to one nested,
not newly hatched,
not fully fledged.

Notes

"Harvest of Ice" refers to 1939's fall. In September of that year, explosive armaments and a massive troop invasion into Poland introduced what the Nazis would do with power: World War II began in Europe.

In "Navy Boys, Montrose, Pennsylvania, 1942," a reference is made to silver dollars. These were placed on the eyes of the dead to keep them closed when the body was laid out for viewing.

"Mercy and 98 Other Names" refers to the 99 names of God in the Islamic tradition. Often used in meditation practices, these names instill in the meditator a particular quality. The first name is All Merciful; the second, All Compassionate.

About the Author

Kathleen Calby, a former communications consultant, metalsmith and singing bowls performer, now writes poetry, tutors, and gardens. Her poems have appeared in *Broad River Review, San Pedro River Review, Willows Wept Review,* and other publications. In 2021, she received a Gilbert-Chappell mentorship with Jessica Jacobs and was named a Rash Award Finalist in Poetry in 2022. She lives in the Blue Ridge Mountains.

Learn more at www.kathleencalby.com.